Love's Epic Poem

part one

I'll write to you
an epic poem
left opened and
unfinished
like never ending
questions
about thinking
about thinking
or the infinite
photons around
us that help me see
how truly, lovely
you are, so I'll write
to no end when we
are apart and I can't
get the thought
of you from my
head,

yet my finite time
compares slight to
forever, but we
the epitome of love
will never be
nevermore,
for after us I ask our
dear reader, the
sons of daughters
and the daughters
of sons to write this
love song evermore
in the style and
verse, rhyme and
meter of the young
producer of this
poem.

Where does this
story begin?
seven years prior, or
seven days
previous?
It's odd, Tori.
Postmodern love
has no definite
erection, though
you think I'm
bashful because I
wrote you a poem,
or 'cause I used the
word erection.

Falling from a fur
tree for a strain on
your back as I slide
down the curve of
your spine, like
Dante descending, I
kiss dopamine
raised bumps of
your skin, so I can
pine for the day
where we make our
start.

I could love you like
a stray bullet in the
arctic smelting a
concentrate of
chemistry. Oh, my
compounded
pounding heart.

I will hold you
sweetly, sincerely,
dearly for a longing
feeling as I find
space in your eyes
and my eyes
partitioned by
prescriptions,
so lovely to finally
see infinity.

Pretty talks, city
strolls, and music
made for us alone to
share in both
elements like
intersecting sets
joined solely for us
to know. Our
perfect union

To sleep alone
in a chair in rows
of academic pews,
though surrounded
by peers, I dream of
the places where we
will be so soon.

Young lovers on a
bus bench
The old man in me
wants to scold them
Yet who am I to say
That their love is
wrong. Perhaps I'm
jealous 'cause all I'd
like to do is to hold
you with your legs
draped over mine
and kiss your neck
while you brush
your hands through
my hair and maybe
we wait for a bus to
head west together,
or maybe we just
caress along the
sidewalk so passing
cars, and passerby
people can see that
when love is right
The rest of the
world feels wrong

Is love the only
absolute?
In a physical world
destined to end
demised by time
and it's ticking hand
to Midnight, might
love be so
immeasurable that
not even doom
Himself could cut
love short.

I thought this while
reading the Prince
of Denmark's fifth,
"Love is begun by
time... passages of
proof, there lives
the very flame of
love."

But in his book, I
think of a certain
player king who I
told you once in a
pretty little thing,
"My love is sized,
my fear is so. Where
love is great, the
littlest doubts are
fear. Where little
fear grows great,
great love grows
there."

What would it mean
In the vacuum of
space,

But I more wonder
what I mean to you
and will you think
well of me after this
poem is through,
and will your love
for me grow so
absolute that our
time no longer can
be measured by
hands or grains of
sand, but in sunsets
spent and sunrises
dreamt. Moments
of a life of love

And what about the
moments... out
in the cold, 13
degree weather
only warmed
by an ember
my quest for fire
sulking on a
cement block
fixated to a phone
tired from unrest
unwell from a
forlorned night
spent drinking
alone and my gut
hurts but not from
drink but from my
sad longing feeling
of missing you...
Yet I'm hopeful
That I'll see you
tomorrow but I'm
glum 'cause
tomorrow hasn't
come.

The thoughts of
your faults....

Now our love songs
remind me of
change. Verses of
songs like loving
you is easy, so never
change a single
thing, or if I asked
you to change
what's the part of
you that I would
miss the most...?

You say you have
faults, but my
impression, or
thought is that your
flaws mark who
you are. Gut
wrenching anxiety,
daytime T.V.
voyeurism, or
a tiny scar on your
jaw make you who
you are....
imperfect, yet
beautiful; flawed,
yes, but truly lovely.

So I could never
scold you for who
you are, and not for
fear of your ridicule,
but as I say it's in
the way you see and
feel the world. Love
and kindness for
humanity, stern
inclination for
those who judge
you, and patient
curiosity for a poet
whose plan is to
spend all the time
with you.

So let's plan to meet
on thirteenth street
and I'll show you
Bellini, and we'll
rip apart the beat-
necks 'cause we
know the only road
worth traveling is
that slow, stroll to
happiness, hand in
hand with the one
you love.

Have I woken from
this dream?
Two nights nearly
past, I slept in your
bed caressed
between you and a
feather pillow. Only
falling asleep after a
heavenly embrace
and woken in the
morn with more
God-like behavior,
but I have to ask
you again, am I
awake? 'Cause to
me it still seems all
too unreal, as if I
can't express
consciousness
of being, but I must
be eyes wide awake
because I write out
these feelings in
blue ink in a green
and gold
notebook....

Last night you told
me in text to dream
of you, so the latter
must be true.
Unless, of course,
I dream within a
dream, a haunting
inception of a
messed-up, loose
perception, but
instead of fear- to
sleep- I'll simply ask
you to pinch me
when you read this,
or
wake me up in
darkness, the
confirmation of my
fear.

That heaven could
make me such a
woman
Oh, tell ho!

It's not much,
really. And I am
happy too. I'm over
the moon happy.
Like I won the
lottery and I'm very
appreciative that
you feel the same
way.

On that heart, you
wrote that you're
always thinking
of me, and
truthfully I think
about you to no
end, so I want to
show you that
through gifts,
through music,
through poetry. But
I'm still trying to
become a better
man
for you, I'm close,
but not yet there.

Sweet lady
I am to be your
sweet boy
until I become your
sweetest man
after I sweep you off
your sweet feet
what joy, what noise
we'll make when I
carry you up the
doorstep.

For now I wait
and prepare my
place and wash my
sheets; for you and
me to rest our neat,
little feet.

The first time you
told me you loved
me, I wanted to
count up from 1,2,3

Four days away
from a spirit
Sunken in a high
chair the beggar is a
king or so I think
for a moment for
my heart is
complete finally
born again in
fortune I am so so
fortunate of your
love....

As I lathered up
chicken in bbq
sauce I am
reminded how I
lathered it up for
you a three course,
two side meal
paired with wine
and coffee too.
I worked up for you
while you dreamt
and slept on my
couch, near the
corner our cozy spot
nestled like
hibernating
squirrels.

Church bells tolling
everything now
reminds me of you
everything now
reminds me to
continue to write
too.

Take the bitter with
the better:
At 8 am I wait for
your love riding an
inbound train to the
south side of town,
but right now my
stomach, tight
sinks more south as
I wait for your reply
like I wait on a
peeking chance of
sunshine on a
cloudy day.

Now, another train,
another minute
Now, another hour
past and still
no answer.

I pass the platform
where I saw you last
where we held
hands under a
parkway and we
hoofed about town
absolutely in love
yet still no answer.
I wonder if you're
sleeping on me
and I only need to
worry about dreams
or are you awake in
your loft making
coffee or tea,
thinking about
loving me, thinking
about telling me
how much you truly
could love me,
but I fear- nervous,
worried curiosity-
I fear you might
want to tell me
something else....

I can pretend to be
happy and paste on
a smile and put gel
in my hair but I
need you to know
that I haven't
experienced so
much joy in one
month as I have
with you. True, no
moment was left
wasted and we fell
in love while
making the bed
your collarbone
coddle, my gentle
touch two parts
made whole a
simple addition
where the result
was infinity.

However, now, left
alone in a city
full of half-lit lights,
I'm lost, unable to
feel the bliss of a
beautiful night. I'm
without wits
just spitting shit
from my teeth....
I'm lost without
you.

I'm alone without
you, here. Do you
feel my tears? Am I
alone in my
melancholy?

And I can't keep
awake I drift in/out
of consciousness
like a lone dingy to
sea so I have
another cup, and
chew on coffee
beans you bought
for me, but I find
the only way to stay
awake is to write
down these
thoughts, they seem
to keep me from
capsizing and
drowning yet I'm
unable to follow a
lecture on Pulitzer,
Thomas Nash,
And William
Randolph Hearst,
so my love I'm left
with this....

Also, I could never
get enough of you.
especially, enough
time.

...God could give me
one hundred years
and I would only
want more, 'cause I
need more. More of
you, more of your
love. More time for
me and you. More
tomorrows, more
good mornings,
more love songs
and more wonderful
words.

Yesterday morning,
I reluctantly rolled
out of bed and
kissed your
forehead
knowing now
another week would
have to come to
past for us to share
a lasting night

Yet instead of being
dreary about my
nostalgia, what if I
could be vitalized
through our
memory, and
genuinely
enthralled
for that moment.

Where should we go
when it's time to
adventure?
Where will we stay
when it is time to
settle?

Oh, God, how I
grow tired of the
city, an isolated
metropolis that
festers with cynics
and businesses.
I miss the country
summers counting
stars under a
blanket of midnight
ecstasy and heaven.

I miss the distant
sounds of speeding
cars and full time
freighters on the
highway.

I miss you, I miss
seeing you home.

City noise pollutes
my ears like a
broken septic tank
at sea. The train
always runs and
chases me and
frightens me
further.

I've never been so
alone, yet
surrounded by so
many faces.
Is this how the
willow tree feels
engulfed and
hidden by the many
mighty oaks?

You are my pine
though different
trees we share the
same roots and I
hope to never love
another as much as
I love thee.

Two nights ago
we planted the
seeds in the most
unfamiliar places
but loved so
tenderly in the most
familiar way.
Thrice we dug out
and hung out
and laid out our
love.

Back to a wet vortex
of tubular metal, I
am sucked to a
vacuum where the
lack of blue clocks
and an
overwhelming
feeling of being
velocitized
somehow freezes
me in space and
time moves slow
or really not at all
which when I'm
with you, time flies
by, way by.

Time is relative to
love not absolute.
Yes, the sun will rise
and surely set, but
at no moment did I
know what hour,
minute, or second
when I saw you last.
Time isn't passed
when you are with
the one you love
time is made
moments are made
and love is made.

Twelve hours later...

I fight sleep on the
same, lame train.
In four days...
I'll kiss the nape of
your neck in
Milwaukee, well,
our rural paradise,
and I will stay
awake while we stay
side by side by
lakeside, along
beach drive but yet
here I write,
well type, on this
elevated plane.
Four full days
and five nights
from your sight,
I ride alone like so
many, but I have
hope for a lovely
wedding.

By this time
tomorrow, we'll be
together, yet it
dawned on me
that springs ahead
and no matter what,
we'll lose an hour.
Lost time spent
with one another
but we'll watch the
stars through your
sunroof thinking
about how the   Cold face, hairless
burning light was   cheeks. Will you
once an eternity   kiss my lips all the
and I'll hold your   same?
hand and wait for
you to kiss me,
which seems like
an eternity

Recognize this bare
expression, my look
for you, it'll never
change. Maybe, you
can fall in love with
me again. See new
life in my eyes.
Remember the first
time we saw the
sunrise, and wonder
if we're still needed
to see the sun set.
What if we woke up
before dawn
and made love
to the dwindling,
lost star, and stayed
in bed till the sun
moved from east to
west, letting it
watch us all the
while.

I once thought a
type of heaven
would be to fly
miles ahead
with your love and
keep pace with the
sun setting or rising
as we head along
together.

At this point, I told
you about my
something heaven
after we spent our
first sunset on the
banks of Lake
Mindoda as it set
over your college. I
held you as my eyes
teary blinked wildly
at the blinding star.

You are more
alluring than warm
weather and I flock
to you like birds
to Florida in
December. My
ticker perpetually
ticks for your love
and every twilight
spent with you
lights up my life.

I'm beginning a new
this week.
Freelanced by
chance, yet I'm here
situated at a long
oak table waiting
for a sign, so for
now I sit and write
out to you, my love.

I saw Chicago, but
then I saw London.
7:00 o'clock in the
U.K. and to the
right Paris almost
eight in the land of
love. I tell you these
times cause I'm
reminded of how
soon we'll be
flying over the sea
to see the former.

When I came to the
room a row
of world clocks
caught my eye
where it laid placed
on the wall.

Soggy socks and a
sprite the smell
moves from my feet
to my face. I send
you photos of
Salvador Dali's
surreal art.

The days are
growing colder as
we're apart. They
say it's spring
but I know spring
won't sprung 'till
our hearts are
pressed in a
warm embrace.
Coffee keeps me
warm for the time
Being, but my cup
cools. It's chilly
waiting in this
weather, yet I'll sip
it cold and swallow
the blackness
because I know
you'll fill me up as
soon as we start.

In 41 days we'll be
abroad, and
I'll lock in your love
on the London
Bridge, or propose
an engagement in
Paris. We'll be the
Americans in Paris
in love with one
another while we let
the city of love
fill our memories
with bliss and
happiness, so a
simple traveler's
story becomes a
tale of two lovers
waiting for the sun.

Hold, hold,
hold on my dear.
I will be coming
home sooner rather
than later. It isn't
my home, it isn't
yours, but it is ours.
Together, a home
for you and I, and
us alone.

I watch the seconds
tick away slowly
and perpetually
ten past four, or is it
three? My eyes pry
past the peripheral
waiting for five.
Waiting for the
clock to countdown,
or is it up?

The binding blue
lines that drag me
along are now
consumed in
swelling traffic that
festers like a pimple
on a dimple that
keeps me in a sort
of purgatory
where there is no
you and the only me
is hungered by
more thoughts of
you. And honey
I'm starving.

Another day in
April
accompanied again
with snow.
My soul
abandoned

With three feet of
bed between you
and me I lay your
head upon the bulb
of my arm and you
press your cheek to
my chest and I
caress the nape of
your neck while you
scratch my flesh
swiping the tip of
your nail carefully
yet tenderly 'till I
kiss your forehead
ever so lovingly.

Only micro-inches,
closing the distance,
as we embrace,
and it is done
as they have done
and we have done
the last thing left to
do.

'Cause all of me
is made for you.

This body only
carries a world
anew and when the
time comes
I will bestow my
soul as holy and
solely for you.

Yesterday night, I
phoned my father,
letting it known, my
ambition to wed, so
to bring you home
and for us to grow
old together, forever
like two snails in
the same tank
slowing our stroll,
yet finding heaven
in our shells.

Fifty minutes past
April's last day,
my stomachs sunk
as I'm left thinking
about you
and what you do.
less than fear
and more than pity,
my memory of
morning chaste
with grace now
haunts and
makes me weird
as I only hope to
hold you while we
articulate like
television static
and speak till we're
fine tuned for
the evening news.
I dread turning off

Please, can I keep
you turned on, so
when I paste my
face to the dark
glass the static
tingles the little,
single hairs of my
upper cheek. Maybe
that's why I'm up at
this hour afraid of
silence, to be alone
and sleep in a bed
without you.

A million and one
so people crammed
safely on a train,
but not a one
could be the one
'cause you, my love,
are the only one.
I know I've done
and said this before,
but when the end
of the train line
comes,can you find
the time to tell me
you love me, hun.

Should I never stop
writing, I wonder
how many times I
reuse the words *you*
and *I*, and *love*, or
even so, but *even so*
I love you.

"Come home,
beloved"

An 80 degree day
ablaze warms my
body to a broil
only cooled by a
breeze of Lake
Michigan winds,
is it such a sin
to love you like hell?
With fire and
brimstone, to fall as
angels fell for a
word more than
love, I burn for you.
To live in a world
wretched and
wicked all for a
moment for my girl
to shake my heart,
and lite my life. To
ignite, to keep mine
and your match
endlessly lit like city
lights or man made
eternal flame. Full
of romance, Full of
flare, Filled with the
ecstasy of our bright
star's blaze.

Button down'd and
dressed up, I hang
my coat on the chair
I sit to write this bit.

Reading
Shakespeare, I am
happily bothered by
the muffed sound of
an old, Hollywood
musical. It makes
me feel like Gene
Kelly, but I know I
smell like Chip
Kelly. My heart
swoons to the
musical tunes
played from an old
tube, and of
course... it reminds
me of you.

Oh, honey.
Let's dance in the
rain and sing in
Paris. I'll take you
by the hand
and spin you to the
rhythm. We'll sway
like Pisa, we'll love
like Rome, and we'll
kiss like only you
and I know how.

Act four scene four,
I could care
less of Coriolanus,
my ears bleed
for this bouncy
noise reverbed from
the other room.

Flowers bloom
I press the smell
of the petal to those
two little nose
holes. Sugar
magnolias *baby's-breath* all so well to
smell but my
protuberance
resonates to sense
the linens and the
perfume of your
perfect place.

I ride so idly
like a baby
rocked to sleep
yet kept up
by sips of black
and sugar packets.
I think about
our last cup...
shared in the
terrace of my
mother's place.

I watched
You ate
I sighed
You cried.

To paint a picture
less than poetic.
Gut-wret jealousy
stemmed from
hectic memories
that aren't mine.

The memories of
youth owned by you
and you alone
as I did not know
you then your
kingdom of
melancholy
your adolescent
adventure lonely
from me, hence my
apparent
unnecessary envy.

These unneeded,
unwarranted
feelings
make my being feel
like a lame duck
mocked in a flock.
Yet I'm seamlessly
unseeming the
strings
to my brain, for
why?
'Cause I need to
want
to hold you as mine.
The idea of you
not seeing me needs
my heart like cat
paws to a cushion
chair.

I vie for this love
and to love like
I never knew how.
To keep my vow
and know you as
forever and now

It is unloving
to be hindered
by a memory.
It isn't love
to not love
the one for
unrequited
reasons of
spite and
jealousy.

I promise to ease
out of my green
insecurity.
To grow up like you
want me to. to
reinvigorate my
love for you, my
hopeful sweetie.
My heart is mailable
but my love for you
is undeniably true.

Sun hidden to a
gray, a last day on
the train. I've gone
to and fro for two
years plus some
more. Now, how
and what I do next
is suspect to you.
what I make last is
first and foremost
in thought of you.
Do I stay adrift in
the city of lights,
do I keep my vow
to kneel by thou
at the ivory tower,
or do I do nothing
and let you decide
whether or not
you wish to stay
by my forever.

I am the arrow of
love you are the
bow.

I am the knob,
but you are the lock.

We are the world
and gravity is the
complexity of love
that complicates,
yet keeps us in
orbit.

Together, you and I
find tulips in bloom
so I hope we hide
amongst the colors
and let our love
cover us forever

Half-out and
hidaway in a coffin
stall in the cellar of
Shakespeare bar,
I try to write to you
some quick poetry
while you wait for
me in a booth of the
same bar.

Americano and
a plate of eggs
with a slab of ham
...I'll have what
she's having

I've drank more
wine than Jules
Verne at a garden
party. You and I
have dined from
London to Lyon,
and we've made
love like honey bees
and peonies, so
sweet a feeling too
soft to sting.

Now, my fiancé.
engaged and at
large abroad.
Et tu es belle.

You're getting ready
in the bathroom,
while I type out my
love, and soon we'll
see the louvre.
Yesterday afternoon
we laid beneath
the Eiffel. They
offered us French
wine and Hors'
devours but already
full and drunk from
love we continued
to lay and watch the
world while we
loved

Ten thousand feet
and three thousand
miles for two
flightless birds
flying high and
riding higher
somewhere above
sometime not said
something done
like two doves
of the same stuff

The sun sets
as we head west.
Miles high, the
Atlantic at our feet.
Our sort of heaven
found by chance
by a cheap flight.
Flying while the
Earth turns about
we keep pace with
her beauty in orbit
Though, the view
Restricted by
the middle aisle
the light leaks
through and I feel
blessed to be
holding you
as the airplane's
wings bring me
and you closer
to home.

You're so sweet
fast asleep
in your airplane
seat

The manifesto of
love songs

Twenty one
hundred
or twenty four
hours past when I
have seen you last
and it's hard for me
to be here, home,
without heart
without her.

My melancholic
turtle heart
retreats to an
empty shell
of a room
left alone
in the black
tar pit of the
back of my mind.
I reminisce
through the digital
photo of the world
we left across the
sea you and me
sitting among the
steps of Albert's
statue. Smiling like
the sweet terrapins
happy to be
away from the
swells and waves.

When you're sad
I am sad
and when I'm sad
you are also sad.

We're learning to
share everything
from microbes to
hotel rooms in
Lyon. it's slight
practice for us to
share a life.

We're spending
more days together
more hours of
weeks with one
another more
minutes and
milliseconds of
seconds shared and
spent with each
other, so this night
doesn't seem right
without you this
night feels like the
end of Revelations.

Sprawled off the
sofa laid out on the
vinyl floor you're
fast asleep I'm
awake with knees
up but we're
together touching
like parked cars
pressing our arms
while linking our
feet before I dream
I wait for you
to kiss me and wrap
me with your
sleeves so I can
sleep next to you
Peacefully

Love is a four letter
word.
Obviously.

Your name is gifted
and solely yours to
own I know you as
you are and I will
know you then,
after now,
after your name
and my name
become the same

As we move forward
together in this life
Please, forever
pull me in
and let me
hold you
like only
I know how.

The many
memories
that await you and
me haunt me like
heaven. One day,
some day, and
hopefully soon
fill my glee visions.

To make a point
to write beautiful
poignant poems
at least one a day
for our next, last
days to be had,
so that my love
can be outlined
and traced for you
our entire life.

I'm amazed yet
crazed by my more
than infinite
love for you.
Finally, we spend
each day
together.
Yet the thought of
losing you
haunts me.

June zooms as our
summer looms
toward warm days
and hotter nights
spent in a yearning
twilight and dusky
evenings in bed
wrapped like a web
and swarmed
with unbelievable
feelings of
peace and ecstasy.

Any fear of love
turned feverish
and lacking that
beautiful quality
that makes love,
love, should be sent
to Hades.

Our love's eternal
flame burns with
the intensity of Hell
and I'll spend a
lifetime kindling
our kindred spirits
and when our souls
flicker or the flame
dwindles I'll recite
poetic verse
and write what
burns or pains my
heart so our ardor
never dies.

The lake
from my left
empty yet blue
breezy but so true
and still so peaceful
that thoughts of you
swim like mythical
fish multicolored
and magical that
jump about high
tide and keep my
mind alive with cool
thoughts of us
floating calmly to
shore sharing
waking hours
forever afloat,
aboard our
collective ship that
skips over
ripples and
waves

When I see you next
I'll give the biggest
kiss 'cause I miss
you like a dog in the
day haplessly
lapping lounging
and napping
dreaming of you
dreaming of you
and me and
dreaming of being
always yours and
happy

Mermaid of my
sheets
the spirit of my
dreams
my morning muse
my evening glee

I love you
like red and blue
makes violet
A new color
brighter and better
but forever
to tint the palette

As to measure love
in quantities and
not the quality or
character is an
impossible task.
I have found
while falling in
love with you
is that love is
immeasurable.
I could write a
thousand words
a thousand
wonderful words
and it would not
begin to quantify
this love for this
feeling of us is
happily complicated
and no other two
same people will
ever know how to
love like how we
loved no matter
how great their
love.

So dear reader
as I make a life
with my soon to be
wife find these
verses and make
them yours and I'll
continue to write to
you, for me, but
mostly for her.

Love never lies
and to never stop
loving you with
so much love...
oh, baby when I
think of you,
romancing you,
my mind numbs
and every song
we've ever sung
plays the playlist
of mine and your
life and I hum like
a honey bee flying
high to the sweetest
melodies in which
words no longer
sound so nice and
the only noise I care
to hear is the silent
presence of our two
souls dearly near
humming like an
A/C in summer
which cooly writes
the love song of a
lifetime only
for us to own

How does a
honey-moon taste?
Well, how long does
it last?
my honey is as
indefinite
as the stars over
earth but a waning
moon makes me
think that nothing
lasts forever....
However,
we may be
honeymooners
but we, the epitome
of ecstasy and
melodies love and
live like no one else
and not even the
moon's phases
could change the
way we feel for us.

When we leave this
honeymoon phase
will you promise to
still behave and
promise to love me
till the grave
because I know it's
harder but I know
you know how
strong we are

May I be ret in
worry- over what?
A lack of financials,
depleting income,
and credit crashing
like cars. Sure, my
sums are something
else, but we will
prosper like salted
peanuts, we are
built to last.

As this takes shape,
I wonder
how soon can we
become wonders of
the millennium,
Invigorators of a
basic generation,
born-again agents
of change who
drape clear curtains
of wisdom over
yellow glasses, so
that when people
look in they can see
that we are who we
appear to be

Cheers to the
happy, weird couple
who are happily
weird together

Life is not a movie
viewed on screen
or acted out like
giant James Dean
life's roll slows and
go's as quick as
your nose grows.

Please, sleep
on my shoulder
over this show
I've seen a
zillion times
'cause the best
scene is between
mine and your head

I think it's the wine
that has you
napped,
fast asleep on my
lap or it's the 12
hour plus day spent
on your feet so
please sleep sweet
my fine, lovely bride
and I'll write this
part so indiscreet
that the day I reread
these lines you'll
wonder how long
you were asleep.

Let it be the second
part where
everything you
might wonder of my
dire heart is known
and sewn like
Moses script on
sacred brick.
This is love's bible
and I know I'll
babble on like
babies talk
but baby this love
is gifted so I need
to write every bit
so when we're old
and wondering
what it was like to
love like two twenty
somethings
in the '20 '20's
we'll flip to
chapter two
of love's
greatest
manuscript

but baby we're
living the best thing
in the world
together and I'd
never change or
leave what we have.
All I have is you and
all of me is for you.
For always, forever.

Here I am to write
again. It's been five
months and we've
done so much
but the feeling of
repeating ideas of
me and you
live with me like
printed ink.

To start writing
again
is to reinvigorate
our love.

I won't say *my* love
as 11 months passed
and each second
makes *our* love into
new shapes where I
am not just in love
with you like crazy.
I am and I love you
now like my own or
our own. To not just
love like a sunset
but to also love like
the moon

To love the moon
more is like to till a
garden in
December. If I
planned better, or
seeded sooner I
might not be tilling
now,but all my fruit
in Autumn tastes as
nice as it would any
day, month or year.

Love is love, which
is love.

I woke from a slack
dream where we sat
on white sands with
our backs to the
waves. I was staring
at a dog asleep,
laying in peace
nowhere near the
tide. You told me
you wanted a
different name you
told me you wanted
to change the world,
so I dug my feet in,
buried beneath
sand, then let rising
waters splash upon
my skin.

When I rolled to my
side in our queen
sized bed I saw you
fast asleep snoozing
to the sounds of a
distant song sung
by the crooning
robin across the
street, half asleep,
in our neighbor's
tree

To write again is
to remember
how we fell in love
we can certainly
spend the time
And I can think it
through I can
remember the day
and second of the
moment that
I saw you.

Unrequited love is
like a song you
heard on the radio
1,000 times. you
know all the words
but you once did
not know any of the
words, so now you
sing them
timelessly without
end over and over
again.

Love is control. love is polite control. We train our bodies and share our souls like exchanging jump ropes on playground blacktop. we take turns jumping rope. It's a beautiful unobservant game of double Dutch

Love is a vehicle toward what we don't know about the world. Like all machines it needs to be kept running well. When a wheel blows out out on the interstate, don't be surprised that the tire popped. All things fall apart but all things can be made whole once more.

Don't say I love you less 'cause I am quiet more.
Don't say I love you less If my smile is not what it was before.

You foolish girl.
I love you
unendingly
like waves to shore.
You are the beach,
you are the stones,
and the waves at
large.

I am the tourist
to your waters and
air, hoping my
holiday
never ends.

I'll always love you
as long as you let
me swim and the
hurricanes don't
win.

The morning traffic
slows to the sound
of my broken car
radio and the
sunrise creeps
distinctly orange
and pink to the east
as I think of all the
things that make
me think of you and
me.

Isolated to the
thoughts in my car.
They hum like The
heater and surge
like a piston. You
stick in my mind as
salt would to the
window shield. I do
not bother to clean
it so the thoughts
grow and grow as I
drive along this
lonely road.

Going through the
motions of a work
week I'm weak and
sick and stomach
pains keep me
seated to an urgent
care chair.
However...
my heart hurts too
but not from the flu.

Last night you
showed me your
doubts as we laid
unable to sleep and
unable to cut the
tension. You
wonder and worry
about me wanting
you, but I can only
tell you so many
times that I love you
completely.

It's time that I show
you, to wake up and
see these words as
gold, goals and
yours.

Come this
November I'll
forever be yours to
hold but just so you
know I always was
and always am.

A year ago in March
we sprung in love
whilst separated by
states. This year we
live like puppies
in a brand new
kennel. To say there
hasn't been growing
pains would be
untrue but to say
that it has not been
full of love would be
blasphemy.

Yes, our love has
idled but it is as
alive as a brand new
battery. I wait for
you to take the
wheel and steer this
vehicle toward the
life made waiting
for us.
The happiness of
love is the wheel
that turns the
vehicle toward are
journeys end.

Writing less, but
living more, or so I
think. April at last
and spring is struck
with such intense
heat that sweaters
and denim
surrender me to
shade. It's a family
day holy Sunday
It's sadly funny
half my family
hardly remembers
me forgetting my
name forgetting
yours too. Though
you know and I
know too that you
and me are
unforgettable.

How many more
words need to be
written, how many
more songs needs to
be sung, and how
many...
I love you mores
need to be said
for you to know
that I love you.

What's the date?
Late April and
6 more months
till we meet
on 2nd street
to be wed
like VW lovebugs
heading west
toward a sunset.

With every chime
that winds that ticks
neatly every hour, is
another second
sooner...
Until we wed in
October

Down and about in
Milwaukee
a neighborhood
with a bay view
close to a church
with a bell too
It rings for me and
you and I know the
sounds that toll tell
us that our love is
sound tells us to get
married soon.

As the season
continues to show
and the vegetation
continues to grow
the grass seems
more and more
colored and the
streets beam with
young lovers.

It's a love song,
and it's pretty
picturesque
but a picture
doesn't do it
justice at all.

As I watch the sun
set and planes
highlight the sky
sitting driver side in
an empty mid size
sedan which feels
largely empty and
echoey 'cause I
don't have you
riding passenger.
It is beauty lost and
views of blue
skipped as each
track plays the
soundtrack of our
love and I feel like a
master of none.
I cringe to the
missed connection
of me and you.

"Like a heartbeat
that drives you mad
in the stillness of
remembering."

Lost in June
I try and keep face
remember that days
are only as long
as the seconds
spent from home.
We're building a
place in a space
which isn't ours so I
can't help but feel
homesick and
sullen like a kitten
spent a night on the
roof.

We dream of the
future and demand
answers too.
Why hasn't
everything
happened in the
way in which we
thought it should?

My mother, our
mother loves us as
she should
and I love you
will always love you
the best I should.

To be continued....

Made in the
USA
Monee, IL